Crazy God Story
(Faith Isn't Blind)

Chris Randall

Cover Art By Calixta Cruz
@nalynnaonline

Crazy God Story: Faith Isn't Blind (Second Edition)
© 2022 by Christopher Randall

This book is dedicated to my wife.
Tricia is the love of my life, and the only family I got to pick. God has used our marriage to teach me how to love.

Without her love and support I wouldn't be the man I am today or know what true love is, and the events in this book wouldn't have happened.

Proverbs 18:22 says that whoever finds a wife finds something good. I've been blessed far beyond what I deserve.

My daughters,
You will always be Daddy's Little Helpers.

To Elise,
You are strong and courageous, always continue to fight for others, even if it means pulling hair. I am proud of you.

To Isabelle,
You are bold and honest. Never be afraid to speak the truth. Jesus said the truth sets us free. I love how you help people and invest in their lives.

To Abbie,
You are adventurous and brave. Your life will be filled with amazing experiences. We are the same person and have some great adventures. You are my little buddy.

4

Contents

The Journal Stories

New Calling Stories

6

Crazy God Story
(Faith Isn't Blind)

Hebrews 11:1 (KJV)
*"Now faith is the substance of things <u>hoped</u> for, the **<u>evidence</u>** of things not seen."*

The Bible teaches that faith isn't blind; that it's based on evidence. Faith is like a door. We may not be able to see what's on the other side of every door God asks us to step through, but we do know Who is on the other side of that door because He continually proves He will always be there.

I hope that as you read my story, you don't see random, individual coincidences but instead see a series of events, orchestrated by God, that were the interconnected building blocks which He used to securely establish and grow my faith.

A long time ago I asked God to give me a life that was unexplainable apart from Him. The following series of vignettes demonstrate how He did that. Typically, when Christians share their testimony, they tell you about how terrible of a sinner they had been before getting saved, and how God delivered them from it all. This, however, is going to be a different kind of testimony.

Sure, I was a terrible sinner; I made a mess of my life through lots and lots and **LOTS** of sinning. Then in December 2008, I surrendered my life to Jesus, and He radically delivered me from who I was by changing me into who I am now. I love that. It's amazing. However, what I want to focus on is what God did with my life in the years following that event because I think it is equally amazing, it will strengthen other Christians, and lead unbelievers to faith.

"How amazing?" you might ask. I have an account on Tiktok where I tell condensed versions of the stories I'm going to share here. I call them "Crazy God Stories" because what God did is crazy amazing. Most of them are stories that only make sense if God is real and supernaturally active in my life as well as in the lives of other people.

I hope that by the time you get done reading this book you will come to understand why I believe that my story would be impossible if there were no God. Not only that, but if you don't already believe in God, I hope your mind is changed. If you already believe in God, I hope that my story bolsters your faith and causes you to follow Jesus with a renewed vigor.

The following short stories are from a very specific time in my life, beginning immediately after I became a follower of Jesus. After surrendering my life to Him, He led me to run a nonprofit mechanic company for several years. I wrote this all down in a journal as it was happening, and now I'm sharing excerpts of that journal here with you.

Aside from Marsha and Scott Jones, the names of the people in the stories have been changed.

The Journal
(December 2008 – October 2011)

December 2008

★ Change

I surrendered my life to Jesus. I was alone at home and didn't say a typical "sinner's prayer." I simply told God I was surrendering my life to Him, and I meant it. Countless Christians over the years shared with me their stories of how God had radically changed their lives when they trusted Jesus to save them, and I believed God would do the same for me if I asked Him to. And WOW, did He!

The death, burial, and resurrection of Jesus had been preached at me incessantly since I was a small child. I had been repeatedly told about how Jesus shed His blood on the cross and conquered death in order to forgive our sin as well as to free us from the power of sin. I knew the Gospel message because I had heard it more times than I could count, but for the first time I put my faith in the Gospel, and at 30 years old God separated me from the sin that separated me from Him.

Until that moment I had been a perpetual sinner who repeatedly tried to change but had been unable to do so. I could change my behavior for periods of time but would always fall back into the same old sin patterns, and it just kept getting worse. I was a lifelong slave to sin until the moment I surrendered to Jesus. Immediately it was as if God reached into my soul, took the DNA of who I was, and changed it. From that moment forward, I was a radically different person, freed from the sin that had held me captive for so long.

I grew up in what I call pseudo-Christianity. I call it that because it was inconsistent and disingenuous; it was flat-out crazy. While I was growing up, none of the adults in my life who claimed to be Christians lived in a way that resembled Jesus, His teachings, His followers, or the New Testament; when I was 18, I asked my mom why I should believe what she did, but she had no answer. I had always wanted God in my life, but no one had ever shown me what it looked like to be an authentic follower of Jesus.

I had read the Bible on-and-off most of my life but never prayed much. This was when that changed for me. Unprompted, I began to read the Bible and

pray every morning. No one told me to do this; I was led to do it by the Holy Spirit. This wasn't just something I did for 15 minutes a day; I spent copious amounts of time everyday reading, studying, and meditating on the Bible. I began using composition notebooks as prayer journals.

I became consumed with getting to know God, learning from Him, listening to Him, and obeying. While I had read the Bible throughout my life, it wasn't until now that I really understood it. I found that the more I dug into God's Word, the more He revealed Himself to me by opening my understanding of the Bible. ◆◆◆

December 2008

★ Family

Of all the changes God made in me, and of all the stories you're about to read, my absolute favorite is the husband and father God turned me into. At this point, I had been married for ten years, and my daughters were 6, 7, and 8 years old. I had always believed that I loved and cared for my family, but I was very self-centered and greatly took them for granted. I was living more for myself than I was for them.

But God changed my heart; He completely broke it down, then rebuilt it. He reached into me, kindled a fire for my wife and children, and has perpetually continued to stoke it. From that day forward I began to love them in a way I never knew was possible. Loving my wife has become one of the greatest missions of my life. If I'm not a good husband and father, then nothing else I'm doing really matters.

I've found that aside from my relationship with God nothing in life is as rewarding as loving my family by living for them daily. My wife is what I most cherish; my relationship with her is my greatest treasure. My children are the most valuable gifts I've ever been given. Every day I pray and ask God to help me love my wife and daughters more; I am constantly looking for ways to do so.

While this may sound like God is secondary to my family, I believe I love and honor God most by placing this type of emphasis and priority on my family. ◆◆◆

January 2009

★ FBC

I was looking for a church home, and a friend recommended that I try First Baptist Church in Rockport, Texas (FBC). I did much more than try it out, I began regularly attending and quickly became very active. I have been substantially blessed to be part of the FBC faith family. God has used my years there to help shape me, train me, and teach me. ◆◆◆

March 2009

★ ARR

I had been working full-time as a mechanic for the six years leading up to my come-to-Jesus-moment but had become unemployed shortly before and was at this time looking for a job. This was when God began to tell me in multiple ways that He wanted me to start a nonprofit mechanic company, using five specific events to do so.

#1) I don't remember all the sermons I've heard over the years, but there was one in particular that God used to kick my butt into action. Scott Jones, the pastor at FBC, spoke in one of his messages about how we shouldn't become spiritual gluttons. If we are being fed spiritually, we must do something with it. When we keep it to ourselves instead of acting on it, we become spiritually stagnant and miss the chance to be used by God. This causes us to be filled with knowledge but no genuine, Bible based experience with God. Instead of growing spiritually, we become spiritually arrogant and unloving. Instead of growing God's kingdom, we become Pharisees who are effective at keeping the lost out of it.

That message hit me hard. I had been spending a lot of time with God, soaking Him in, and this sermon overwhelmed me with the idea that I needed to live out what I was learning, but I had no idea what that would look like. I was unemployed and had been concerned about finding gainful employment. God began speaking to me that He had a specific plan for me that would incorporate both of those things; He was preparing me for a job that would glorify Him. He would pour out of me what He was pouring I n to me.

#2) One morning I was reading the Bible, and God spoke to me very plainly through Ephesians 4:28 (NKJV), which says, *"Let him who stole steal no longer, but rather let him labor, working with his hands what is good, that he may have something to give him who has need."* One of the main things God delivered me from in December 2008 was being a liar and a thief; that had been my identity. I was the type of mechanic that gave all mechanics a bad name.

Immediately after I read that Ephesians passage, God told me that He wanted my new job to be fixing cars for broke people for free and that I was never to ask anyone for money. I instantly began to ask God questions and confess my concerns to Him. Because I had only been a mechanic for six years, I didn't have the tools or knowledge to run a mechanic business. My biggest concern was how would I earn money to support my family.

#3) I have a wife and three kids which means I have a responsibility to provide a place to live that includes electricity, plumbing, beds, and of course, food. How was I supposed to do that when God wanted me to work for free? That was when God led me to Matthew 6:31-34 (NKJV),

> *"Therefore, do not worry, saying, 'What shall we eat?' or 'What shall we drink?' or 'What shall we wear?' For after all these things the Gentiles seek. For your heavenly Father knows that you need all these things. But seek first the*

kingdom of God and His righteousness, and all these things shall be added to you. Therefore, do not worry about tomorrow, for tomorrow will worry about its own things. Sufficient for the day is its own trouble."

God very lovingly told me that providing for my family would be His responsibility; that I only needed to trust and obey Him. I had always wanted God in my life and continually tried to follow Him on my own terms, but I always held back just a tiny part of myself. However, when I surrendered my life to God 3 months prior, that all changed. You see, what I figured out after 30 years was that if you try to follow God on your own terms, then you really aren't following God at all. That leads to a frustrating, exhausting experience that leaves you broken.

Romans 10:9 (KJV) says, *"...if you confess with your mouth that Jesus is Lord and believe in your heart that God raised him from the dead, you will be saved."* When it says, *"...confess with your mouth that Jesus is Lord..."* it's a statement of surrender. You are saying that Jesus is your Lord, that He is your master. Your life does not belong to you anymore. Throughout the gospels, Jesus repeatedly said that you couldn't follow Him if you don't die to yourself. It is impossible to follow Jesus while living for yourself at all.

Throughout my life I had repeatedly surrendered 99.999% of myself to God, while always just holding on to a tiny .001% of myself. There had always been a minuscule part of me that I just wouldn't let God have, and the truth is that the .001% habitually kept me in a cycle where I always took back the other 99.999%, leaving God 0.0%. Before December 2008, I had never truly surrendered my life to God. I was faced with a real test. Had I surrendered to God this time, or was I going to resume control?

#4) I decided that I would obey. My immediate dilemma was telling my wife what I believed God was telling me to do. I will never forget the day I had the conversation with her about the possibility of me working full time and intentionally getting no paycheck. This was probably the scariest thing I have ever done in my life. If you are a married man, I dare you to tell your wife that you want to work for free. I had envisioned about a thousand bad ways this conversation was going to go for me. However, after telling my wife what God was calling me to do, all my fears were alleviated. Before I could tell her why I believed this was what God wanted for our family, she calmly told me to wait for just a minute, because she wanted to show me something. She got up and walked into the other room, returning with her Bible.

She sat down and told me that she wanted to read me something that God had shown her recently. She opened her Bible and read Ephesians 4:28. *Ephesians 4:28!!!* She agreed starting a nonprofit mechanic company was what God wanted me to do. I was blown away. I was expecting a lecture about the insanity of what I was thinking about doing, but instead got confirmation in the form of my wife's blessing!

#5) While I believed God was calling me to start a nonprofit mechanic company, I still had some doubts. I had been a very dishonest person for 30 years, and it was possible, even likely, that I was seeing events through the lens of lingering guilt over previous transgressions and somehow was trying to make amends for my past. I told God that I would absolutely obey Him, but I wanted to make sure this was truly Him and not some delusional idea of my own design.

A few days after that, Steve, a local pastor I knew called me and asked if I could look at a car for Frank, one of his parishioners. I got to Frank's house I found that he had a mid-90's Chevy and the engine had thrown a rod. That means his engine was impossible to repair. Frank then told me that before his engine died, his car already had a litany of other problems. Not only had the transmission been slipping, but both the alternator and the power steering pump were shot.

Frank's car needed thousands of dollars' worth of replacement parts, but he had no money. He had lost his job in January due to a lack of transportation. He was so broke that he would walk around town to different convenience stores, take smoked cigarettes out of the ash trays, and use whatever tobacco was left to roll his cigarettes. Neither one of us had the money to buy the parts Frank needed. When Steve asked me to check out Frank's car, his church had intended to pay for the repairs if the total cost was less than a few hundred dollars, but they just didn't have the kind of money necessary for a major repair. There was no way possible I was going to be able to help Frank.

Three days later my brother (whom I hadn't spoken to in about a year) called to tell me he was moving and that someone had abandoned a car at his house six months earlier. He wanted to know if I wanted the car because it had to be moved ASAP, but he couldn't afford to have it towed off. As of yet I had only talked to my wife about what I was planning on doing for a new job, so my brother had no idea. Because I hadn't been to his house or talked to him in such a long time, I had no idea he had this car stuck there. What's amazing is that the car my brother wanted me to take away was a mid-90's Chevy that had the same engine, transmission, alternator, and power steering pump that Frank's car needed.

It was like God took a megaphone and loudly declared that the idea to start a nonprofit mechanic company was 100% from Him and that He would take care of all the details, including my family's finances. Fixing

Frank's car was the birth of Affordable Auto Repair, a full-service, nonprofit mechanic company "...dedicated to sharing the love of God by offering free auto repair to those in need." (That's what was printed on my business cards)

During the repair of Frank's car, I shared Jesus with him. I figured that since God was demonstrating His love for Frank in such a big way, that he would gladly receive the gospel. However, I became somewhat discouraged when he did not want to become a follower of Jesus. I figured that God was going to save tons of souls through what I was going to be doing: that He was going to do big things. Frank rejecting Jesus weighed on me heavily.

The following Sunday at church I was in a life group, and one of the leaders randomly started talking about how he and his wife had moved all over Texas. He said that everywhere they lived, they always planted pecan trees but never stayed long enough to reap any nuts from any trees. He talked about how we won't always see fruit from what we do, but that we must follow Jesus and trust the results to Him.

I was blown away because this story was unprompted and had no relevance to anything else we talked about that morning, yet it was exactly what I needed to hear.

After fixing Frank's car, poor people kept coming to me in a steady stream to get their cars fixed. I worked on everything anyone brought me, never once asking for money for the work that I had done. ◆◆◆

June 2009

★ My Wife's Job Part 1

By the time June rolled around, I was working five to seven days a week, eight to ten hours per day, fixing cars for free. While I never asked for money, people would occasionally give me small donations. These donations typically averaged a total of around $200 per month.

My wife had been working at a convenience store for several years, but we both felt as though God wanted her to quit. At the time, she had no other job prospects, and we didn't have any other substantial income source. However, our family took a step of faith, obeyed God, and my wife resigned from her job. ◆◆◆

July 2009

★ The Rent Check

Our rent was due on July 1, and there was a grand total of $358 in our checking account, leaving us $292 short of what we owed for rent. Our landlord demanded that rent be paid on the 1st of every month, and not a day later.

My wife and I spent some time in prayer and believed God wanted us to write a check to our landlord for the entire $650. I wouldn't normally write a check I can't cover, or recommend that anyone else do so, but we were confident that it was what God was telling us He would cover the check we couldn't and wanted us to trust Him that He could.

Immediately after dropping off the rent check that we couldn't cover to the landlord I received a phone call. Someone wanted to hire me to repair the AC on two vehicles. They offered to pay me very well for the work, refusing to let me do the job for free. I made enough off that job to cover our rent check, pay all our monthly bills, and stock up on groceries.

While God had been clear that I was never to ask for money, He taught me through this experience that there would be times when He would send me people like this that were His provision for my family. ◆◆◆

July 2009

★ The Tape Measure

I was driving down the highway one day and saw a vehicle on the shoulder with its emergency flashers on. Since I was in my work vehicle, I decided to stop and see if they needed help. The driver had stopped in order to use her phone and didn't need any assistance. As I was walking back to my car, a tape measure fell off the back of a truck. It was a 25 foot Stanley Fat Max. The fall left a few minor dings, but overall, it was still in great working condition.

As a mechanic, I seldom need a tape measure, and when I do something basic and inexpensive is more than adequate. What fell off the truck was a bit on the high-end side of tape measures. Dave, a buddy of mine, was working as a house framer, and I thought that he might be able to make better use of it than me. When I called Dave to ask him if he wanted the tape measure, he was shocked. I didn't know it, but two weeks prior, his tape measure had broken, and he had been borrowing one from his boss. He had been unable to afford to buy a new one.

Right before I called Dave, his boss had reprimanded him for not having bought his own tape measure yet.

Dave was a Christian who worked with a bunch of guys who weren't. His coworkers spent copious amounts of time trying to get Dave to sin in any way that they could. When Dave told his coworkers about the tape measure, they were in disbelief. They kept telling him that it must be broken, that I couldn't possibly have had the Cadillac of tape measures just fall off a truck and remain in perfect working condition. They were dumbfounded when they discovered that they were wrong.

For Dave, this was God letting him know that He was with him while being persecuted by his coworkers. I was blessed to see God at work. ◆◆◆

August 2009

★ Trip To My Sister's

After paying rent on August 1, my family was broke. I had several jobs lined up, but no money was coming in, and my wife had still not found a new job. Around the beginning of the month, I received a phone call from one of my family members in Louisiana. Their employer had a Ford F250 that had broken down, and the dealer wanted around $5,000 to fix it. They offered to pay me about half of that if I would drive over and do it.

I was told the diagnosis of the truck, so I could order the needed parts and have them delivered to where I would be doing the work. After arriving, I discovered that I had been told incorrectly what engine the truck had, which meant that I had to reorder the parts. Originally, I had planned on driving over one day, fixing the truck the day after, then driving home the next day. However, the new parts took five days to come in.

My unexpectedly extended time in Louisiana ended up being a huge blessing. I had been working up to 70 hours per week, and I needed a break. Not only did God use this job to provide needed finances for my family, but He also provided me with some necessary rest.

Through this experience, God taught me that I was trying to do too much and needed to slow down. ◆◆◆

★ Schlitterbahn

Around the end of the month, I did some work for a man who ended up giving me five free tickets to Schlitterbahn. His wife worked for a radio station, and they had some extra tickets to give away. Not only was God regularly providing for my family's needs, but He was showing His love for us by doing exceedingly abundantly above what we had imagined or asked for (Ephesians 3:20). ◆◆◆

October 2009

★ My Wife's Job Part 2

After several months of being unemployed, my wife landed a job as a property manager. In addition to her salary, we were given a free apartment, our water was covered, and the property owners paid the majority of our electric bill. We live in a small town where decent jobs are very scarce. Having no steady income for five months was a little nerve-racking, but God was teaching us to wait on His timing. A common expression is "God waits until the last minute," but I believe what's more accurate is that God waits until the best minute.

God gave my wife a job that helped sustain the ministry He had given us and was also opening many more doors for ministry. ◆◆◆

October 2009

★ A Place To Work

I typically went to people's homes to fix their cars, but occasionally logistics made the job difficult or unsafe. Having a place to work became a continual challenge that God was about to solve before I even started looking for a solution.

One of the pastors at my church asked me if I could replace the rear end (the thing that makes the rear tires turn) in a truck for a lady who was a deaf-mute if the church bought the rear end. I was happy to do it, but her driveway was soft sand. When changing a rear end without a lift, you need solid ground like asphalt or concrete in order to be able to do the job safely.

When I told the pastor that I didn't have a good place to work on the truck, he offered to let me use the church parking lot. The parking lot wraps around most of FBC, and I thought they would want me to work out back, away from the road, so as not to make the parking lot look like a big mess. I'm in south Texas, and it gets hot and humid. The heat index in the summer always climbs into triple digits. In the front of the parking lot are several big trees that provide ample shade. I was told that I should fix the truck up front in the shade. After fixing the truck, I was told that I was

more than welcome to use the shaded part of the church parking lot anytime I needed a place to work. ◆◆◆

October 2009

★ Redbook

I tried to stay busy, but I would sometimes go days without work. I ended up doing a job for the grandson of a man who owned a phonebook company. He liked what I did for his grandson so much that he gave me a free quarter-page ad for AAR. This increased my business so that from then on, I always had a steady flow of work.

For me, having more customers had nothing to do with money because I wasn't working for money. What I loved about having more business was that it meant more opportunities to share the gospel with people. The people I worked for were almost always shocked that I legitimately didn't ask for any money in exchange for the work that I did for them.

This provided me with numerous opportunities to demonstrate God's love in a way that demanded an explanation, leading to numerous gospel conversations.

If you want to be effective at reaching the lost, you need to say and do things that require a reaction from people. Instead of just telling the gospel to people and then asking them for a response, create situations that require them to respond to the gospel and interact with it. That's the example Jesus set for us and it's extremely effective. ◆◆◆

October 2009

★ My Car Broke

My car died while I was driving down the highway. After coasting onto the shoulder, I called Jake, a friend from church, to ask for help. He was about to get off work not far from where I was stranded, so he picked me up and helped me to push my car onto a side street. The plan was to go to Jake's house, borrow his truck, and rent a tow dolly to pick up my car.

Before that happened, a young man named Travis came out of a house near where I had parked my car. He told us that the neighborhood we were in had a high crime rate and that he would keep an eye on my car for me. Jake and I were both convinced that I needed to share the gospel with Travis.

After returning to my car, Travis and I got to talking. He had grown up in a religious home, but he had never heard the gospel. I shared the good news with him, and he gladly gave his life to Jesus.

Having your car break down on the highway sucks but look at the amazing results. If my car had broken down 20 feet sooner or farther than where it did, I would have left it in a different location. I believe my car broke down exactly where it did because God wanted someone to meet Travis that He knew would share the Gospel with him.

This event demonstrates how much God wants to reach people with the message of salvation, to seek and save the lost. It also demonstrates that the bad things that happen to us aren't arbitrary. It's easy to get frustrated when stuff goes wrong, but it takes faith to look for where God is working in that situation. ◆◆◆

November 2009

★ Casting Crowns

I had fallen in love with the music of Casting Crowns, and they were doing a concert that I wanted to go to. It wasn't something I could afford; however, a local Christian radio station was giving away several pairs of tickets. All week I unsuccessfully to win a set.

The last pair of tickets was given away about two hours before the show. About thirty seconds later, one of the DJs called me on the phone and told me that they had one pair of tickets for the second row as well as some backstage passes that someone had won but was going to be unable to use. He wanted to know if I wanted them. YES! I was very excited.

My wife didn't want to go, so I went with one of my friends. Matt Redman opened! At one point during the show Mark Hall asked the crowd a question, then without warning or prompting he stuck his microphone in my face to get the answer! We got to hang out with the band after the concert! It was a glorious night! I love

how God loves to bless us out of the
blue. ◆◆◆

February 2010

★ The Truck

I got a call from Jeff and June, a couple who were helping support a single mom. The transmission in her car had gone out, and they wanted me to install a used one they bought from a junkyard. They ended up getting three transmissions because the first two were no good! Yes, I swapped it out three times.

During the course of the job, Jeff asked me what church I worked for. He was under the impression that I was a full-time pastor at a church and that fixing cars for free was something I did on the side. When I told Jeff that AAR was my full-time job, he was flabbergasted.

At the time, I was driving a 1990 Mazda 626 that had seen much better days. It was the car that had broken down on the highway. Jeff and his wife decided I needed a work truck and bought me a 1995 F150 that was much more conducive to my job.

A few days after getting my truck the engine in my car blew up. God's timing and provision is always perfect. Often, He doesn't provide what we need until after we've walked by faith into obedience. ◆◆◆

★ Drugs

One day while driving to a job, I saw a truck stuck on the side of the road with a flat tire. I stopped and found that Richard, the man driving the truck, had a spare tire but didn't have the tools to change it. While changing his tire I talked to him briefly about the gospel, but the conversation didn't go anywhere. I gave him one of my business cards and wrote on it the name, address, and phone number of a local church I like, and went on my way.

Several weeks later, I received a phone call from Josh, a man who attended the church I had mentioned to Richard. He wanted to buy me a cup of coffee the next time I was in town but didn't give me any details as to why except to tell me he wanted to talk to me about Richard.

When I met with Josh, he told me that Richard had been stuck on the side of the road for several hours when I stopped to help, and that I was the only person to do so. Richard had been a drug enforcer for a living. He was the person who made sure that drug dealers got paid or bad things would happen. When when his tire blew out, he had a gun in his truck and was on his way to kill five guys he was working with.

Richard had been wanting a change in his life, and the fact that after hours of being stuck on the side of the road the only person that stopped to help him mentioned Jesus shook him so deeply that he went to the church I recommended and there he met Josh who shared the gospel with him. Richard gave his life to Jesus, was radically changed, and got out of the drug business altogether.

Richard and his girlfriend had several small children. If he had gone through with what he was planning, he almost certainly would have wound up dead or in prison.

I believe that God caused this man to have a blowout and kept anyone else from stopping to help him before I showed up because God knew I would plant a seed. God is constantly at work in the lives of people to bring them to Himself. In Luke 19:10, Jesus said that he came to seek and to save those who are lost. God is still doing that today, and He uses us when we allow Him to.

In Matthew 4:19 (KJV) Jesus said, *"Follow Me, and I will make you fishers of men."* He was making a promise to everyone that He will transform anyone who follows Him into someone who naturally leads people to Him. God will do amazing things through the life of anyone who is surrendered to Him and follows Jesus by faith.

Jesus said in John 4:35-38 (NKJV), *"Behold, I say to you, lift up your eyes and look at the fields, for they are already white for harvest! And he who reaps receives wages, and gathers fruit for eternal life, that both he who sows and he who reaps may rejoice together. For in this the saying is true: 'One sows and another reaps.' I sent you to reap that for which you have not labored; others have labored, and you have entered into their labors."*

We don't have to lead everyone to Christ, but we are all called to plant seeds as frequently as possible. God has amazing plans for those seeds. God rewards our obedience with opportunities to be obedient and sometimes gives us glimpses into the amazing ways He uses our obedience to impact eternity. ◆◆◆

★ My Jack

I used to have an undersized floor jack that I limped by on, but it wasn't sufficient for the work I did. One day I was about to leave for work but found that my jack had been stolen. I was pretty upset because I didn't have the money to replace my jack, and it's tough to work as a mechanic when you don't have a jack.

Later on that same day I was unexpectedly given money for my business by someone who I had done a job for. It was enough money to buy a full-size jack that was adequate for my work. ◆◆◆

May 2010

★ STCH

One day while at the grocery store, I ran into John, one of my friends I hadn't seen in a long time. We decided we should reconnect and meet up for coffee. John called me the following Saturday and told me that his daughter's car had just broken down and that if it wasn't moved by Sunday that it would be towed on Monday.

Sunday afternoon I went and looked at the car and found that there was nothing wrong with it. It had overheated because of a loose hose clamp, but when I checked it out the hose clamp that was loose was in fact nice and tight. Their car had certainly broken down, but what made it break down shouldn't have done so. It would soon become apparent that God had orchestrated this little fiasco.

After getting the car back to John's house, we got to talking. He shared with me that he and his wife had been thinking about becoming house parents at a place called South Texas Children's Home (STCH), which is a Christ-centered group home. To do so,

49

they would have to leave their careers and sell their home.

John and his wife each had great jobs, as well as a beautiful house. The entirety of both of their families had been telling them that they were ridiculous to consider giving up all of that security. I shared with John how amazing it had been for me to live by faith and about the adventure God had me on because I chose to walk by faith and follow Him.

God was calling John and his wife to work at STCH, but every one of the voices in their lives were trying to drown out the voice of God. They needed some confirmation. Often God connects us with people who need to hear our story because of how it relates to their life. They may be in the middle of something that we've already walked through with the help of God, and consequently, God uses our story to help them find Him in theirs. ◆◆◆

June 2010

★ Two People

At the apartment complex my wife and I lived at for her job, there were many broken, hurting people. Drug and alcohol abuse were the norm, as were broken and blended families. My wife and I were the only couple that were in our first marriage and had no children outside of our marriage.

Two different men at different times approach me and asked me how to fix their lives. Both had been watching me and my wife. They saw that we had a strong family, we were always helping people, and had no addictions. One of the most common activities around the apartments was to sit around with the other residents and complain about their significant others. My wife and I never did that. In fact, when women started bashing on their men, my wife talked me up. When these two men looked at my life, it looked to them like I had it all together.

Both men shared with me how messed up their lives were due to cycles of substance abuse and poor life choices. They both had tragic stories

51

and were looking for a change. I shared the gospel with both; neither accepted it. I was glad to be able to at least plant some seeds. While I didn't get to lead either of the men to Jesus, it reminded me of how much change God had brought into my life. I'm hopeful that others will water the seeds I planted and that one day those seeds will produce fruit. ◆◆◆

September 2010

★ Dead Truck

I had an electrical short in my truck which destroyed several wiring harnesses and expensive electrical components. The total cost of parts was several thousand dollars more than I had, so I ended up selling the truck.

Because my wife and I were living in an apartment, I couldn't work on people's vehicles where we lived. We had a family car, but my wife needed it for her job. Since we had no other vehicle, I wasn't sure how I was going to get to work. My job outlook may have looked bleak, but I wrote the following in my journal:

"My truck is a toast at the moment - I have no idea what direction my life is about to take -- BUT I know God is in charge - I have seen Him work countless times in the past and come what may He is sovereign."

Years earlier, I would have panicked over the situation I now found myself in, but God had been so active in my life, that I was confident that He had a plan. Within a few days, one of my neighbors, Tommy, who lived about a half mile from my apartment, asked if I ever needed a place to work. He owned his house and had a large driveway with a garage.

When I told Tommy about my current truck predicament, he told me that I could set up shop at his place for as long as I needed to. God came through yet again! My new work location was only about a 12 minute walk from home. Even before my truck (which I'd only had for eight months) died, God had already prepared a solution. ◆◆◆

December 2010

★ Christmas Money

The rest of the year went by uneventfully; my wife and I kept working and ministering to people. My wife had become very involved with sharing the love of Jesus with the residents at our apartment complex.

When December rolled around, we didn't have any money for presents for our kids. About a week before Christmas, I had two different men I'd previously done work for give me money to buy presents.

God always has a plan to take care of us when we follow where He leads. ◆◆◆

February 2011

★ Family Car

My wife's car had catastrophic engine failure requiring substantially more money for repairs than we had. Not only that, but it had developed a lot of other expensive repair needs. With very little money in savings, we simply trusted that God would provide for us. A week later, one of my friends told me he was selling a 1985 BMW 325E in nice shape and offered to sell it to me on payments.

Several days after getting the car, someone hit it in a parking lot. Fortunately, they had insurance to pay for the damages. The adjuster looked at the damage and cut us a check. The actual repairs cost much less than the estimate. I had made a small down payment on the car, and the leftover money from the repair was enough to pay off the balance. ◆◆◆

April 2011

★ The Guitar - Dave

One of my favorite activities is playing the guitar, and I have been blessed to have a beautiful vintage Seagull S6 acoustic electric. It's about a $600 guitar that I traded some extra tools for. On the Sunday before Easter, God told me to give my guitar to my buddy Dave (the tape measure). Dave is a phenomenally talented musician who was on our church worship team. He didn't own his own guitar but had been borrowing one.

As soon as God told me to give Dave my guitar, I immediately began to argue with Him.

"I can't afford to go buy another guitar; what am I going to play?" I asked. God responded by telling me not to worry about it. I wrestled with it all afternoon and into Monday but eventually decided that I would obey what God was asking me to do. He had never led me astray before, and I didn't believe He was about to start.

Before giving my guitar to Dave, I thought I would discuss it with my wife. At the time, she was at my sister's house in Louisiana, helping my sister get ready for her wedding. I called my wife and told her I believed God wanted me to give my guitar to Dave. The truth is that I was hoping she would tell me I was an idiot and that we couldn't afford to buy me another guitar. I was planning on obeying God, but honestly, I wasn't happy about it.

My wife told me that I should go ahead and give my guitar away and that my sister had a guitar she wanted to give me that she said was "really nice." I was blown away. I called Dave after talking to my wife and asked him to stop by after work. There were two guitars he had always wanted: Gibson and Seagull, and I gave him my Seagull. He was mass stoked. After arriving at my sister's house for her wedding, she presented me with a beautiful 1970 Epiphone acoustic guitar. It had been stored improperly for many years, so it did need some repair work, but overall, it was a cool guitar that sounded great.

In 2016 the repairs to the Epiphone failed, and I had to replace it. I ended up buying a cheap $50 pawn shop beater.

Early in 2019 Dave had asked me to help him with a vehicle repair. While we were working, he told me that his wife had bought him a new Gibson guitar for Christmas and asked if I wanted the old Seagull back.

I am constantly amazed at how God rewards our obedience. Whenever He asks us to give something up, He always has something better in store. That doesn't mean that if He asks us to give up a material item that we will always get a material upgrade. Sometimes the better thing is simply getting more of God by experiencing Him which causes us to know Him more intimately. ◆◆◆

April 2011

★ The New Truck

The BMW my wife and I had was very small, quite a bit too small for a family of five. One of my friends mentioned to me that he had seen an ad on craigslist for a nice truck that the owner wanted to trade for a small, sporty car. The truck was an extended cab with plenty of room in the back seat to fit our kids. I called the owner of the truck, and he was excited to check out my car. We ended up doing an even swap, our BMW for his truck.

One of my favorite parts of doing mobile auto repair was that almost anytime I went to work on anybody's vehicle, they would stand outside and talk to me while I worked. This gave me continual opportunities to share the Gospel with the lost, as well as the chance to minister to those who were saved. Basically, if I worked on your vehicle, you were going to hear about Jesus and get prayer.

While I was thankful that God had provided me such a convenient place to work, I found that most people dropped off their car or had it towed to me, reducing my opportunity to minister to people. Trading our tiny BMW for a truck was not only better for our family, but it allowed me to go back to doing mobile auto repair, which gave me many more ministry opportunities.

I Had been praying for God to provide me with a physical shop because I had always thought that it would be more beneficial to what I was doing, He showed me that was not the case. Sometimes God gives us what we ask for to show us that what we think we need is not as good as what He provides. ◆◆◆

June 2011

★ My Wife's Job Part 3

In May, my wife had left her job. Initially she was supposed to work Monday through Friday from 8:00 a.m. to 5:00 P.M. and occasionally work half days on Saturday. Eventually, her bosses had her working seven days a week. When she resigned from the apartment complex, my wife had no job prospects. But after much prayer, we believed that God wanted us to take a step of faith, that my wife was supposed to leave her job, and that God had a plan.

With no safety net but God, my wife quit her job. Her last day was May 31, 2011. Since we were still living in our apartment, it meant that we would have to pay rent by Friday, June 3. She had one paycheck still coming, but she wouldn't get it until after rent was due. For the week leading up to our rent being due, I had no work that was going to pay me any money. We weren't sure how we were going to pay our rent, but we were certain God would take care of us.

The Sunday before our rent was due, I was talking to one of our very dear friends, Marsha, and told her what was going on. I told her that I didn't want her to tell anyone, or help us in any way, or even get people to pray for us. I shared our situation with her because I was confident that God would take care of everything, and I thought that by bringing her into this scenario, she would get to share the experience with us of God doing something amazing.

Friday rolled around, and BAM! I got a call from a man who needed some work done. Not only was he refusing to let me do the job for free, but he wanted to pay me in advance that very day. The amount he was paying me was much more than we needed for rent. He had no idea what my financial situation was, but God did!

With this money coming the exact day we needed it, some people would say that God had waited until the last minute, but I believe that's a mischaracterization of how He works. I believe that God waited until the best minute. Survived adversity causes strength, the greater the adversity, the greater the resulting strength. By God coming through in the eleventh hour so frequently, it causes our faith to grow much more than if He had come through at the onset.

When I called Marsha to tell her how God had provided, she told me that she had nervously been praying all week. This was substantiated evidence that our faith in God was valid, and I think it left her in awe of God and His presence in our lives. ◆◆◆

June 2011

★ Meds

My daughter was on some expensive prescription medication for epilepsy; without insurance one month of refills was over $1,300. Every six months, we had to renew our insurance, and when we did it would typically lapse for about three weeks. By the end of May, we were out of my daughter's medication, and the last day of May was when our insurance would end. For most of June, we would have no insurance, which meant we would not be able to afford the meds.

A few days before the end of May, we tried getting a refill sent to the pharmacy, but her doctor's office didn't get it sent over until June 3. By the time the prescription arrived at the pharmacy, our insurance coverage had expired. I felt an urge to just go ahead and try to pick up her medication, and trust that God would work it out.

Boy, did God come through! When I went to pick up the prescription, it was covered by our insurance company. After I got home, I checked to see if our coverage was still current; it wasn't, it had ended on May 31.

When you follow God where He leads, your problems are His to figure out, and He faithfully does so in awesome ways. ◆◆◆

July 2011

★ Rent

I wasn't sure how we would pay our July rent until a check came in the mail from the IRS days before our rent was due. There had been an error on our previous year's taxes, and they sent us the difference, which was more than enough to pay our rent. ◆◆◆

July 2011

★ My Wife's Job Part 4

My wife applied for and got a job with the local high school. This job allowed us to keep up with our rent and other bills. ◆◆◆

October 2011

★ My Shoulder

I spent a lot of time working in children's ministry, and one day we played dodgeball. The next morning, I couldn't raise my right arm. After multiple visits to two different doctors, they both concluded that I had torn my right rotator cuff. The insurance we had only covered our kids, which meant that I couldn't afford the surgery I needed.

The prognosis was that I wouldn't be able to do mechanic work anymore. My time with AAR as my full-time job was over. I wasn't sure what God had planned for my life going forward, but He had taught me to live by faith. By this point, He had proven His existence through extensive evidence.

While I was no longer running Affordable Auto Repair, God wanted to show me fruit from the seeds I had planted. ◆◆◆

October 2011

★ Brake Job

A few weeks after I hurt my shoulder, I got a phone call from Josh, a man I had done some work for about a year earlier. The front brakes were going out on his van, and he wanted me to fix them. I was about to tell him I wasn't going to do it because of my shoulder, but God whispered in my ear that I needed to take this job. Fortunately, the brakes on Josh's van were incredibly simple, something I could literally do with one arm tied behind my back.

When I worked for Josh the first time, I didn't talk to him about Jesus at all. He was hanging out in his house with some of his friends, and they were all drunk. I was guessing that God wanted me to fix Josh's brakes so that I could share the gospel with him. I spent time praying and preparing to share the gospel with Josh before he arrived.

When Josh arrived, before I could say anything to him, he looked at me and told me that I had changed his life. Even though I didn't talk to Josh about Jesus previously, he knew I was a Christian. On the back of my business cards, it states, "Affordable Auto Repair is dedicated to sharing the love of God by offering free auto repair to those in need." Josh told me that he and his wife had never seen a Christian who would do something like what I had done.

They were so blown away that they found a church, started taking their kids, and all of them got saved. Their lives were radically changed. I just can't overstate the importance of sowing seeds and trusting God with the results. ◆◆◆

October 2011

★ Drunk

I ran into Tom, a man I had done some work for in 2010. While working for Tom, I shared the Gospel with him, telling him about the change God had made in my life. We had a great conversation. He didn't get saved, but he said he wanted to meet with me later to talk more. I tried several times to get hold of him, but he was always unavailable.

Fast forward to 2014. I saw Tom again and he told me that when we met the first time, he had been an alcoholic and that he had almost lost his marriage as a result. He kept trying to quit drinking but was unable to do so. He remembered what I had told him about how God had changed me and freed me from my sin. That caused him to find a church and give his life to Jesus. As soon as he did, he was freed from alcoholism, and his marriage was restored.

He continued going to church, his life kept changing, and he became a much better husband. His wife, who was not a Christian, was so amazed by the change in her husband that she started going to church with him to support him. Eventually, she also gave her life to Jesus.

This brings us to the close of an amazing chapter in my life. Ever since I started following Jesus in December 2008, my life has been full of stories like these. While AAR played a huge role in my faith journey, it's not the cause of the amazing things God did through my life. I've had many people falsely believe that God worked through my life in the situations that He did because He gave me an abnormally special calling to run a nonprofit mechanic company.

Jesus said in John 12:24 (WEB) *"Most certainly I tell you, unless a grain of wheat falls into the earth and dies, it remains by itself alone. But if it dies, it bears much fruit."* The truth is that while God isn't going to call most people to run a nonprofit mechanic company as their full-time job, He will use whatever gifts we have to do God-sized things when we die to ourselves, surrender to Him, and follow Jesus by faith.

In most of the stories I've shared, God didn't do amazing things through me because I ran a nonprofit mechanic company. Look back at my stories and see that God put me in the right place at the right time to meet with specific people because He knew I would be faithful to sow seeds. The rest of the stories I'm about to share are a testament to that. ◆◆◆

New Calling

My time running Affordable Auto Repair as my full-time job ended when my rotator cuff tore, but God wasn't done with me. It took several years for me to be able to effectively use my right arm again, and I was eventually able to return to work. However, I didn't return to AAR full time; instead, I got a job as a mechanic at a local shop. My new calling from God in life became being a Godly husband and father and working a typical job to support my family.

Loving my wife and kids and modeling for my daughters what a godly husband and father looks like has been the greatest journey I've ever been on. It has been my favorite, most cherished adventure. While this may seem a lot less exciting to some people than running a nonprofit mechanic company, I assure you that God's activity in my life has not decreased at all. He has continually led me to amazing faith experiences that anyone could have.

You don't have to have huge faith or be called to something extraordinary in order to see God work in extraordinary ways; you only have to follow Him by faith. Even small faith is adequate faith if it causes you to act (Matthew 17:20). I'll give you a few examples of that. In the following stories, I was just a regular Joe Christian, living by faith, following Jesus, yet still experiencing God in amazingly powerful ways.

June 2012

★ Prison

Bill Glass Prison Ministries travels to prisons around America, sharing the Gospel with inmates. They have speakers share their testimony with groups ranging from several dozen to a few hundred prisoners. Those groups then break up into smaller groups of twelve or less, and volunteers meet with them and share the gospel.

One weekend I went as a volunteer to two prisons in Beeville, Texas, and I've never experienced spiritual warfare in such a physical, tangible way. As I walked into the first prison, I was overcome with the sense that I shouldn't be there, that I needed to leave. For the first few hours, all I wanted to do was flee as fast as I could and head home. It was overwhelming, palpable, and demonic.

After we met with the first group of the morning, we had a break, and I ended up in the prison's chaplain office. As I walked in, I could feel the presence of the Holy Spirit. His presence was so thick in that room that you could touch it. There were inmates who worked in the chaplain's office, and their faces were visibly radiating the love of Jesus and the power of the Holy Spirit. The moment I stepped through the door into that office, the presence and power of darkness that had latched onto me and followed me around all morning fled in terror from the presence of the living God!

I left that office overflowing with the Holy Spirit. Over the next day-and-a-half, God used me to lead fifteen men to salvation. ◆◆◆

June 2012

★ Kenya Part 1

I went on a ten-day medical mission trip with my church to Mombasa, Kenya where the population was roughly 80% Muslim. The area we were in was third world, and most of the residents within a few thousand miles had absolutely no access to health care. Our group consisted of two doctors, several nurses, and about a dozen general volunteers. We gave free medical care to anyone who showed up. We treated hundreds of locals who had a wide range of medical maladies.

Because we were a Christian group the Muslim leaders in the area did not want their people to visit us, but because of the dire need for medical care, they allowed it. These patients were strictly warned by their leaders that they were not allowed to talk to us about anything other than their medical needs, especially not Jesus.

During the time we were there the members of our team were constantly asked by locals why would choose to leave America in order to come to give them medical care. They did not understand why we would leave the comforts of America for their destitute their area of Mombasa. Over 150,000 people in Mombasa live in slums without sanitation, healthcare, potable water, or sewage. About 50% of the population is positive for HIV/Aids. We were holding our clinic at a church in one of the slums.

Every time someone asked one of our group members about why we had traveled across the world to help them, they got the same answer; they were told that we were there because God loved them, and we wanted to share that love with them. This baffled them because they spent their entire lives afraid of their god, Allah. They had been taught that not only is Allah angry, temperamental, and could punish you at any moment for any reason he saw fit, but also that Allah does not care for anyone individually.

They had never heard of a God who loved and cared for them and wanted to know them personally. Hearing about the God who loved them for the first time and seeing that love demonstrated through us had such a profound impact that at the end of the week, 58 Muslims gave their lives to

Jesus and were baptized. If 58 Muslims getting saved doesn't seem like a big deal to you, then you don't understand what it cost them. A Muslim in Mombasa who gives their life to Jesus is almost guaranteed to not only be disowned by their family but to also lose whatever livelihood they have. Fifty-eight people well knew the likely consequences of following Jesus. They considered the cost and were won over by the love of God.

This experience felt like something right out of the pages of one of the gospels. While Jesus wasn't physically present, the body of Christ (the church) was. It was just like all the times in the Bible where Jesus rolled into town with His entourage, did some Jesus-sized stuff, and people started following Him because they had experienced His love and compassion. God loves to work through His church. You miss out on getting to see God work when you aren't part of a church family. ◆◆◆

June 2012

★ Kenya Part 2

One night during the mission trip God put a huge burden on my heart that I needed to talk with Katheryn, a girl that was part of my group. I didn't know her well, and I had no idea at all what God wanted me to talk to her about, but I obeyed anyway.

The next morning, I walked up to Katheryn and started a conversation with her. I was blown away because almost immediately I began speaking to her about very specific things in her life that I couldn't have possibly known anything about. Without her saying anything I brought up some major decisions had been wrestling with and told her what God wanted her to do.

Katheryn was shocked and began to cry. The night before she had been praying about the exact decisions which I had just finished talking to her about.

I had obeyed the Holy Spirit and He spoke directly to Katheryn through me. By faith I stepped into the opportunity God created, and both Katheryn and I experienced God.

The things we read about in the book of Acts and 1 Corinthians 12 are still happening today when we live by faith and obey God. The Holy Spirit has not stopped working through His people in amazing ways. ◆◆◆

September 2014

★ Glasses

One day I needed to get a new pair of glasses and went to one of those places that make your glasses in about an hour. My youngest daughter was with me, and we wanted to tell someone about Jesus, so we briefly prayed for the opportunity before going into the store. While we were waiting, we tried talking to one of the other customers about the gospel, but he made it very clear he wasn't interested. We didn't have an opportunity to talk to anyone else until a salesgirl helped me with my glasses.

The store was very busy, so while she was helping me, there just wasn't time to share the gospel. I mentioned God to her briefly, but she didn't have time to talk about Jesus. After picking out my frames, my daughter and I had about an hour to kill while waiting for the store to make my glasses. We decided that while we waited, we wanted to find a Bible to give to the salesgirl and ended up picking one up at a local Christian bookstore.

After we returned to the store to pick up my glasses, while I was checking out, I handed the salesgirl the Bible we had bought for her, and she burst into tears. She told me that she had wanted to find a Bible but didn't know where to buy one. Since the store was still very busy, she didn't have time to talk, but I believe that God intentionally had me and my daughter encounter her that day so that she could encounter Him.

God is constantly at work in the lives of the lost to show them their need for Him. We cross paths with these people regularly, and if we are willing to step out in faith, we will get to see God work in remarkable ways. Before I handed the salesgirl the Bible, I was worried that she might get upset and offended. I had no good reason to believe she would be receptive. But here's the thing, the idea to give her a Bible didn't come from me or my daughter; it came from God. Before seeing her reaction and hearing what she said there was no way for me to know that the idea was a burden placed on my heart by God. My daughter and I acted out of faith and found that we

were getting involved in a place God
had already been working. ◆◆◆

June 2020

★ Sheds

I had to buy two custom sheds for work, and the man delivering them didn't have some of the materials necessary to install them properly. I took him to the hardware store to pick up what we needed, and on the way out, he ogled what he felt was an attractive female. He noticed and was shocked by the fact that I intentionally did not join him in checking out the woman. In surprise, he asked why I didn't check out women, which he felt was "normal male behavior."

I told him that I don't do things that will dishonor my wife, regardless of whether or not anyone sees. I continued on and explained that "normal male behavior" demeans and degrades women. This led us into conversations about Biblical marriage and what being a godly husband looks like, followed by the fundamentals of being a Christian. You see, he's saved, but no one has ever really taught him what it looks like to follow Jesus. He left with a new hunger for Jesus.

Sure, I left out a bunch of years between this story and the others, but I wanted to show you that Jesus has continued to work through my life as I've followed Him by faith, and to encourage you that He will work through the life of every-day regular-Joe Christians who do the same. ◆◆◆

The Present

Since December 2008, I've continued to live by faith and follow Jesus. Sometimes it's HARD and scary and painful, and He drags me along while I kick and scream, but He loves me, and it's beautiful, and it's worth it. The journey is continually changing direction, often veering _far_ off the course I thought it was heading down, but I find that Jesus is always with me, leading me, and patiently waiting for me to follow along.

When things get rough, I think of Jesus and the disciples crossing the Sea of Galilee in Mark 4:35-41. While Jesus was sound asleep in the back of the boat, a storm arose that threatened to sink their tiny vessel. When Jesus didn't do anything except continue to sleep, the disciples frantically woke Him up, and in a panic asked why He wasn't concerned about their imminent doom.

Jesus stood up and commanded the storm to stop; it immediately obeyed. He then called the disciples knuckleheads for being scared and asked why they had no faith. These men had been traveling around with Jesus, watching Him perform radical miracles, but when things got scary, they listened to their fear and forgot their faith. When life is at its worst, I try to remember what God has done and press on in faith. But sometimes, I'm like the disciples, and I freak out, and I toss my faith out the window.

Thankfully Jesus wasn't done with His disciples after the Mark 4 incident; they hit a bump but carried on. They continually screwed up again and again and again, but Jesus was ***never*** done with them because no matter how big or hard they failed they always continued on by faith.

Faith is a journey of following Jesus. It doesn't matter how many times we stumble, how hard we fall, or how big we fail, the journey continues if we get up and just keep going. That's faith.

You will stumble, fall and fail in glorious, gigantic fashion, but to Jesus it's nothing more than a pause before you continue on your journey together.

The Norm

I believe that God wants the stories I've shared to be the type of God encounters that all believers regularly experience. In Matthew 4:19 Jesus _promised_ that He would transform anyone who follows Him into someone who naturally leads people to Him. Ephesians 2:10 (NKJV) says, "*For we are His workmanship, created in Christ Jesus for good works, which God prepared beforehand that we should walk in them.*" God had a plan for your life even before you were born. He has amazing adventures prepared for the two of you that He wants you to experience. Those experiences with God always cause you to know Him more intimately.

The amazing things we see God doing with people's lives throughout the entire Bible aren't limited to people in the Bible. God didn't stop doing miraculous things through people after the Bible was complete. He is still at work today in the lives of regular, everyday people who are surrendered to Him, living by faith, and following Jesus.

Hebrews 11 has been called the hall of faith. It is a list of screwed-up people who God used in amazing ways that were impossible apart from Him. This list contains people who were disobedient to God and at times doubted Him; there were liars, murderers, manipulative cons, sexually immoral people, plus a whole bunch of other messed up individuals who did jacked-up stuff. All the people on this list were failures in life; they were massive sinners who most people would say were beyond redemption.

The one thing that all these people had in common was faith; it's what God looks for above everything else and when we have it then it's what He always sees instead of our failures. When we see these people's stories in the Old Testament, we observe how badly they messed up and perpetually blew it. However, what we see is very different from God sees. Hebrews 11 is His opinion of them, and what we see there is that God was concerned with their faith and not their mistakes because He viewed all of their actions through the lens of their faith. The pathways of their faith journeys were littered with inadequacies and sins that were overcome and trampled by their faith. In each of their lives, faith was a fire that in God's eyes burned away each and every one of their sins, faults, and shortcomings, so that the only thing left for Him to see was obedience: the victory of faith. To God, their failure no longer existed because it was destroyed; completely erased by their faith.

The God we serve is Living and *POWERFUL!* He spoke everything that exists into existence. He made a donkey talk. He made the water in the Red Sea stand up like a wall. He kept three men who stood in a blazing furnace from being harmed by the flames. He closed the mouths of lions for Daniel. He caused Peter to walk on water. He gave Sampson superhuman strength. He used Elijah to raise the dead and Elisha to cure a leper. He used a teenage boy to defeat a literal giant. He made planet earth stop moving so that Joshua could win a battle. Throughout the Bible God continually worked *POWERFULLY* for and through His people far more than what I've listed here.

Jesus said that when the Holy Spirit comes and lives inside of a person, that the person would receive *POWER* to be a witness for Jesus (Acts 1:8). The Holy Spirit comes and lives inside of you the second you are saved, and at that moment, the *POWER* of God lives inside of you because God Himself lives inside of you. That means every single person who is born again has God Himself living inside of them.

The *POWER* we see God exercise through the folks in the Bible is the exact same *POWER* that He wants to exercise through every believer.

The reason God exercised His *POWER* through the lives of people in the Bible is because they acted by faith. They acted because they believed that God exists, they believed what He said, and they believed He would respond to their faith (Hebrews 11:6). In response to their faith, God exercised His *POWER* through their lives and in the world around them.

God will exercise His *POWER* through the life of any and all born-again believers who follow Jesus by faith. Stay with me, as we explore what that looks like.

95

Change Your Thinking

When was the last time you listened to a missionary talk about the work that God had done through them in some remote part of the world? Places like the plains of Africa or the heart of the Amazon rainforest or in a small group of ramshackle villages somewhere in the Himalayas or on a hurricane-devastated coastline or an inhospitable third world place with a high crime rate or a region where Christianity is illegal, and the missionaries could be imprisoned or even executed if the wrong people found out they were there.

When missionaries head back to America from parts unknown, they usually share their stories. They speak in churches, on podcasts, in newsletters, and on many other platforms, and tell their own Crazy God Stories. When Christians hear these stories, they are frequently amazed. They hear of God-sized things being done in foreign lands, then look at their own lives, and to some extent, feel disillusioned.

Disillusionment may not be the conscious thought in the hearer's mind, but somewhere deep down inside, they feel a disconnect. They hear the missionaries' amazing stories, stories that are the type of things you read about throughout the pages of the New Testament but that we seldom see in America today. When we hear about Bible-type stories that are currently happening "over there" we wonder why we don't see them happening here.

This disconnect is even greater for many who have gone on short-term mission trips. A friend of mine, Jill, who was a relatively new believer, went on a three-month mission trip to Uganda, Africa. While there, she regularly saw God use both her mission group and the local church to do the types of things that we read about in the book of Acts. Jill experienced God daily and was constantly in awe of Him.

Upon returning home to the United States, Jill quickly became confused and frustrated. The things from the Bible she had seen God regularly doing in Africa weren't things that she ever saw Him doing in America. It appeared as though Crazy God Stories only happened on the mission field, and once she got back to the states, she was no longer on the mission field, so the amazing work of God ceased.

Jill didn't understand why she didn't see God working through the church in America the way she saw Him work through the church in Africa and she became very disheartened; almost depressed. This is the same type of disconnect people experience when they hear stories from missionaries. Why do we hear about God doing things on the mission field that we see in the pages of the New Testament but don't see God do those things at home? WHY???

The problem is our thinking, which shapes our expectations in such a way that it limits what God is *willing* to do through us. We hear stories of how God works miraculously on the mission field and think that the mission field is the only place God works miraculously. Sadly, we've been deceived about where the mission field is, about who God considers to be missionaries, and about who God is willing to work through in crazy amazing God sized ways.

Matthew 13:54-58 (WEB) *"Coming into His own hometown, Jesus taught them in their synagogue, so that they were astonished and said, "Where did this man get this wisdom and these mighty works? Isn't this the carpenter's son? Isn't his mother called Mary, and his brothers James, Joses, Simon, and Judas? Aren't all of his sisters with us? Where then did this man get all of these things?" They were offended by him. But Jesus said to them, "A prophet is not without honor, except in his own country and in his own house." He didn't do many mighty works there because of their unbelief."*

Did you catch that? The reason Jesus didn't perform almost any miracles in His hometown was *because of their unbelief.*

Except for His hometown, everywhere Jesus went, He did copious amounts of miracles on a regular basis. Numerous people saw those miracles and told others about them who in turn told even more people. News of Jesus and His works traveled through Israel like a wildfire. Every time Jesus entered a new town, everyone who needed healing of any kind would find Him. If their infirmity prevented them from getting to Jesus, then friends and family would either carry that person to Him, or they would ask for Jesus to come to where the sick person was. These types of actions were a solid demonstration that people believed in Jesus, and He never refused to heal anyone who came to Him in belief.

The people in Jesus' hometown had listened to the same stories about Jesus that the rest of their nation had heard, they even saw Jesus do a few miracles, yet they chose to disbelieve what they heard and saw in regard to Jesus. As a result, almost no one came to Him for healing or sought healing for others. Their actions were evidence of their unbelief. It proved they had no faith.

The reason Jesus didn't do many miracles in His hometown was that the peoples' lack of belief kept them from coming to Jesus to do anything supernatural in their lives. Jesus was present, willing, and able to display the power of God to those who came to Him because of their belief, but when people didn't come to Him it was evidence of their unbelief. He responded to their lack of belief with a lack of action. Their disbelief was a choice.

Many people throughout the Gospels chose to not believe in Jesus regardless of how what evidence they had. The chief, most tragic example of this is Judas Iscariot. He spent the better part of three years with Jesus and saw every miracle, sign, wonder, and God-Sized thing Jesus ever did. He had a front row seat to some of the greatest evidence for Jesus in history, and yet Judas CHOSE to not believe in Jesus. The evidence that Judas chose to not believe in Jesus was Judas' betrayal of Jesus.

Judas was not an isolated example of disbelief in the face of evidence. In John chapter 11 many people saw Jesus raise Lazarus from the dead. In verses 45-46 we see that multiple people chose to disbelieve in Jesus regardless of seeing firsthand what He had done.

The gospels are filled with many more accounts of other people who chose to disbelieve despite any and all irrefutable evidence.

Belief is always a choice. You decide what you will or won't believe, including whether or not to believe God. For some people no amount of evidence will ever be enough to convince them to believe.

In the gospels, Jesus always responded with action to those who sought Him by faith. Conversely, He responded with inactivity (and frequent criticism) to those who had no faith. You see, their actions were a direct result of what they believed.

God rewards everyone who's belief causes them to diligently seek Him (Hebrews 11:6). In the gospels, Jesus healed all those whose belief caused them to seek healing from Him and didn't heal any whose lack of belief kept them from seeking healing from Him. Action demonstrates belief, while inaction demonstrates disbelief (see James chapter 2).

God wants to reach the lost in America just as much as He wants to reach the lost in the rest of the world. He wants to work through American Christians in the same way that He works through overseas missionaries; the difference is belief.

Overseas missionaries are constantly living in a way that demonstrates that they believe that God will work through them in the same way He worked through Jesus' followers in the book of Acts, and God responds by doing what they believe He will do. So often in America, our actions demonstrate opposite beliefs of our overseas missionary counterparts, and God responds to us in the same way that Jesus did to those in His hometown.

When we think of missions, we typically picture somewhere "over there" as the mission field and assume that missionaries are the people who move away from here to go live "over there" on the mission field.

Many of us who don't fit into that definition of a missionary consider our daily lives to be separate, distinct things from missions. If we want to get involved in mission work without moving "over there," we go on local or short-term mission trips.

The problem with that is that God views every square inch of this planet as a mission field, and every born-again Jesus following Christian a full-time missionary.

Did you know that in God's estimation every place on earth with unsaved people is a mission field, and that every follower of Jesus is a missionary? If you are a Christian, but haven't been called to overseas missions, then you are a God ordained full-time missionary, and that where you live is the mission field God has called you to.

We are sojourners on a pilgrimage in this world (1 Peter 2:11). This world is not our home. Our citizenship is in heaven (Philippians 3:20). Jesus came to this world to seek and to save the lost (Luke 19:10) and has tasked every one of His followers with the same mission (John 20:21, Matthew 28:18-20, Mark 16:15-16, Luke 24:47-49, Acts 1:8). This was God's plan for you; His will for your life before you were born (Ephesians 2:10). No one who is saved is excluded from this plan.

Whether you are a mechanic, a cashier, a florist, a doctor, a stay-at-home parent, retired, or any one of a bazillion different vocations your job and your neighborhood and your social circle and the people you meet on a daily basis are all your mission field.

God wants you to be a full-time missionary exactly where you are.

1 Corinthians 7:20 (NET) says, *"Let each one remain in that situation in life in which he was called."* After you get saved you don't have to wait for God to give you a task or mission or calling on your life to start seeing Him at work in and through your life. God may call you to do something specific at some point but until then He wants to work as mightily through your life where you are just as much as He does in the life of the most entrenched foreign missionary.

You don't need to go to Bible College, enter vocational ministry, or become a missionary abroad to be able to see God use you. You simply need to believe that He will use you exactly where you are and then act on that belief. God will respond to your faith with action.

In my last job I managed a fleet maintenance department. Through my work I interacted with hundreds of people on a regular basis - coworkers, employees, bosses (I had roughly 9 of those), vendors, and customers. Most of them didn't know Jesus, didn't go to church (and weren't willing to), and had no interaction at all with my pastor or anyone else in vocational ministry (including missionaries). The only way any of these people were ever going to hear about Jesus, was if I and the few other Christians who worked with me believed that we were missionaries to these people and acted on that belief.

It is the responsibility of every Christian to engage with the people they encounter in both Gospel actions and Gospel conversations. They are our full-time mission field. God wants to work through us localy to reach the lost just as powerfully as He works through foreign missionaries to reach people in other countries.

I believe that and I act on it. God responds to that faith by doing crazy amazing God things that look like something from the book of Acts. Most people think I used to be a mechanic for a living, and they are right. But that was just my vocation. I was also a fulltime undercover missionary with a ministry habit who became addicted to experiencing God at work. It's a habit I've never been able to kick, and I wouldn't want to even if I could.

Faith

Hebrews 11:6 (MEV) *"And without faith it is impossible to please God, for he who comes to God must believe that He exists and that He is a rewarder of those who diligently seek Him."*

Without faith it is impossible to please God. That is intense. How do we know the difference between claiming to have faith, and actually having genuine faith that pleases God? What is the evidence of faith? Think back to the people in Jesus' hometown and switch the word belief to faith.

James 2:18-20 (NKJV) says: *"Show me your faith without your works, and I will show you my faith by my works. You believe that there is one God. You do well. Even the demons believe—and tremble! But do you want to know, O foolish man, that faith without works is dead?"*

While Hebrews 11:1 tells us that faith is based on evidence, James takes it a step further and tells us that there will be evidence of our faith. What we believe will be demonstrated by our actions; we act based on what we chose to believe is true.

When we live by faith, not only is God pleased with us, but He also rewards us! I hope that my story has been an example of that. The hall of faith (Hebrews 11) exemplifies this.

If you were about to sit in a chair but thought it looked sort of rickety, you might decide to stand instead of sitting. If you chose to stand, you could claim that you believed the chair would hold you, you might be convinced that you believed it would hold you, but the truth is you don't really believe the chair will hold you. If you genuinely believed the chair would hold you, then you would have sat in it. You have zero legitimate faith in the ability of the chair to hold. Dead faith doesn't sit in the chair; living, active faith does.

The only thing that God asks of us in return for all that He has done for us is to have faith in Him. Everything that we do in obedience to Him is evidence of our faith. When the Bible gives us guidance or instructions, we do those things as a result of faith.

Loving others, forgiving people, praying, following Jesus, sharing the Gospel, and everything else that goes along with being a Christian is either an act of faith or the result of faith.

According to James, if your faith doesn't produce actions, your faith is disingenuous, dead, and worthless. If you think I'm harsh, open your Bible and read what Jesus said in Luke 14:25-35; He didn't pull any punches. Jesus regularly spoke this bluntly because the eternal destination of people is at stake.

Living faith will always produce obedience to God because if you genuinely believe God, it will be the cause of your actions. However, for us to obey God, we must know what it is that He wants us to follow. The only way to do that is to listen to Him and hear from Him.

If you want to follow God by faith, but aren't sure how to listen to listen to Him, or what He wants from you check out Romans 10:17 (NKJV): *"So then faith comes by hearing, and hearing by the word of God"*

Instead of saying "the Word of God," some translations say "the Word of Christ" or "the Message of Christ." Ultimately, what this verse is telling us is that faith is an obedient response to hearing what God says. Faith = listen to God, chose to believe what He says then obey Him.

2 Timothy 3:16 teaches that the Bible is a supernatural book breathed out by God; it is God speaking directly to us through human authors. If you want to hear what God has to say to you, then you must read the Bible.

The most discussed topic in the Bible is God; He is mentioned tens of thousands of times in the pages of scripture. The second most talked about thing in the Bible is the Bible itself and its importance in our lives. The Bible mentions itself over 1,000 times. The longest chapter in the Bible is Psalm 119 (176 verses), and it speaks exclusively about the necessity of the Bible in a person's relationship with God. The Bible makes it clear that the Bible itself is as essential to our relationship with God as breathing is to living.

One of my friends from Tiktok says that God is only silent when your Bible is closed. If you are literate, have access to the Bible, but you don't read it, then you are ignoring God and not listening to Him. You are refusing to have a relationship with Him.

If you want your faith to grow then read the Bible; really soak it in, meditate on it, study it, talk with others about what you've read, and journal about it. You will find that God begins to communicate with you through this. Be willing to respond in obedience to whatever God says to you. If you are afraid that you may not be willing, ask Him to make you willing! Spend time in the presence of God in prayer, ask Him to prepare your heart to hear Him, and to give you the faith to respond in obedience. *I believe one of the key reasons God doesn't speak to us is because He knows we won't listen or obey*.

Jesus said in Luke 6:45 (NKJV) "*...out of the abundance of the heart the mouth speaks.*" What you take in the most is what will shape your thoughts, beliefs, and ideas (Romans 12:2); and that is what will determine your words and actions. When we read the Bible with the intent of setting aside personal bias, listening to God and accepting what He has to say to us, the Holy Spirit changes us from the inside out so that following God (living by faith) is a natural byproduct. It changes us so much that we transition from struggling to try to figure out how to do

Christianity, to following Jesus being so natural that it's harder not to do it than it is to do it.

Personal Bias includes things like our feelings, preconceived ideas, personal experience, and what others have taught us. All those things get in the way of us hearing what God has to say to us because they cause us to see what we read through the lens of our own personal truth which is at odds with God's truth. Personal bias is a mute button to the voice of God.

God often tells us things that don't line up with our personal beliefs or lifestyles. If you want to hear from God, then you must listen with the intent of submitting to what He says regardless of what you think or feel. Since God is the source of all life and truth (John 14:6), and His thoughts and wisdom are as far above ours as the heavens are above the earth (Isaiah 55:9), then we need to accept that when God tells us something that contradicts our worldview it ***ALWAYS*** means that we are wrong 100% of the time. What God says is always 100% true whether we like it or not.

When we listen to God and obey Him that is active, living faith. God always rewards our faith by *proving* that He is faithful and that our faith is not misplaced. This causes our faith to grow and empowers us to trust God even more. This is a beautiful circle. Listen to God. Obey Him. Then He gives you evidence that He is faithful, which causes your faith to grow. The more you trust and obey God, the more you will be able to trust Him.

This is what Paul was teaching us in Ephesians 2:8 when he wrote that faith is a gift from God that doesn't come from ourselves; it is not something we can produce or grow on our own. While faith is a gift from God, He doesn't simply just have faith appear in us out of nowhere. He continually gives us opportunities to choose faith; to act by faith. Those opportunities for faith are the gift! When we act on them our faith grows.

Paul called faith a gift, meaning that it's something God freely offers to us but that we have the choice to accept or reject. We constantly have two choices; walk by faith or walk by sight (2 Corinthians 5:7). We can choose faith by trusting and obeying God, or we can live by what we see, think, and feel. When we choose faith, God grows it and gives us more, and we come to know God more intimately in a way that is impossible apart from faith. When we don't choose faith, we distance ourselves from God.

When the storms of life try to blow us away, a person who has not lived by faith is much more likely to walk away from God than a person who has a solid foundation of faith. Not living by faith causes us to have weak faith that crumbles easily. When we exercise our faith, God strengthens it and gives us faith that can withstand the worst that life can throw at us.

The Bible, prayer, and obedience to God have a symbiotic relationship in our faith that we have briefly looked at in this chapter. We are going to break these three things down a bit more in-depth so that we can better understand how they interact together in our lives to produce faith.

Follow Me

When you read my story, it may appear as though I had multiple, individual acts of faith. The truth is that my story is just one continual, singular, unified, lone act of faith that shows up at different times and in various ways. That one act of faith was deciding to follow Jesus.

Think of electricity in a house. One power line supplies all the electricity to the house. However, there are multiple places where we see the electricity being used: light bulbs, TVs, ceiling fans, fridges, phone chargers, water heaters, and air conditioners. While all of these are individual, isolated uses of electricity, they aren't disconnected from the rest of the electricity in the home. They are all the same electricity, from the same source, just displayed at different times and in different places, for different purposes. Faith is like that.

When you start following Jesus, you begin walking by faith on a journey of faith. As long as you are on that journey you don't use faith one minute, then plug along for a period of time without using faith until the next time faith is required. No, you are constantly, without ceasing or pausing, following Jesus by faith.

In Matthew 4:19 (NKJV), Jesus said to two fishermen, *"Follow Me, and I will make you fishers of men."* What Jesus said to Peter and John was a radical promise that He was making to everyone. Jesus was telling us that if anybody follows Him, He will transform them into someone who naturally leads people to Him.

Churches today spend countless amounts of time, money, energy, and other resources trying to reach the lost, trying to grow, and trying to stay relevant. Yet when you look at the modern church, you see shrinkage. People are walking away and leaving the church in increasing numbers.

A cursory search of the internet shows that church attendance numbers have plummeted over the last 30 years. The studies I've looked at say that two-thirds of kids who grow up in a

Christian home end up leaving the church somewhere between the time they enter high school and graduate college. The church is losing people substantially faster than it adds new believers.

So, what's the issue? I believe that the church today too often focuses on programs and methods and marketing and strategy, but it overlooks that God's only plan for reaching the lost and growing the church is following Jesus and making disciples who make disciples. That's God's plan A, and there is no plan B.

About 80 years ago, A.W. Tozer said that in the first century, if the Holy Spirit had left the church, 95% of what they were doing would have stopped; but if the Holy Spirit left the church today, we would continue doing 90% of what we were doing and not even notice He was gone. That's a fair assessment and it is scary how true it still is.

Jesus made a radical promise to everyone willing to follow Him in Matthew 4:19; when we look at verse 20 we see that Peter and Andrew's response was also pretty radical. It says that they *immediately* left their nets to follow Jesus. They did much more than just walk off the job that day, we see in Matthew 19:27 that they left *everything* to follow Jesus.

Leaving everything wasn't a crazy whim. Jesus said in Luke 14 that anyone who doesn't hate their entire family (verse 26), die to self (verse 27), and forsake everything they have (verse 33) *could* *not* be His disciple. That sounds crazy, and it is radical, but what does it mean? Was Jesus telling us that the wacky, homeless guy on the street corner who wears a sign proclaiming that the end is near is the only one who got it right?

Nope. Not at all. When we look at the Gospels and the Book of Acts, we see that genuine followers of Jesus had spouses, owned homes and businesses, worked 9 to 5, and raised their kids in homes with white picket fences (metaphorically). So when Peter claimed that they had left all of that and everything else to follow Jesus, what did he mean; how did he follow through with all of the things Jesus said in Luke 14?

Romans 10:9 (WEB) says, *"If you will confess with your mouth that Jesus is Lord, and believe in your heart that God raised Him from the dead, you will be saved."* Confessing that

Jesus is Lord doesn't simply mean that we say "Jesus is Lord" and then everything is copacetic. By calling Jesus Lord, you are surrendering your life and control of it to Jesus; you willingly become a living sacrifice (Romans 12:1). Even your decision-making belongs to God.

In John 12:24 (NKJV) Jesus said, *"Most assuredly, I say to you, unless a grain of wheat falls into the ground and dies, it remains alone; but if it dies, it produces much grain."* For Jesus to be your Lord, you must die to yourself. You cannot simultaneously live for yourself and follow Jesus. It is only when you've died to yourself that your decision-making belongs to God.

December 2008 is when I began following Jesus. I surrendered my life to God, and the Holy Spirit began working in my life immediately. The first thing that happened was that He changed me and freed me from the sin I had been trying unsuccessfully to quit for years. After that, He began leading and directing my life. All my experiences with God that I've talked about so far have been a result of the fact that all of the decisions in my life have belonged to God.

Some of those decisions have led people to believe that I am a bad husband and father. Fixing cars for broke people for free instead of working a normal job with a regular paycheck led some people to accuse me of being a poor provider. To them it looked like I hated my family! That's what Jesus was talking about in Luke 14:26.

Over the years, I've heard many Christians tell stories of times when they clearly knew God wanted them to do something, but they didn't obey. They knew that God wanted to do something through them, but for any number of reasons (fear or being too busy are just a few examples) they passed on the opportunity.

Ultimately the core reason is a lack of belief: they chose to not believe God just like the people in Jesus' hometown chose not to believe Him.

Without exception, these stories always end in regret. People regret that they didn't obey God and consequently missed out on getting to see Him work and do something amazing. They regret missing out on experiencing God.

Jesus promised that if I would follow Him, that He would transform me into someone who naturally leads people to Him. He makes the exact same promise to *everyone*. When I surrendered to God, it meant that following Jesus wasn't an optional part of Christianity for me to choose because it is God's definition of what a Christian is! As I followed Jesus, the Holy Spirit continually changed me to be more of what He wanted me to be, and God just kept using me to lead people to Jesus. Jesus did with my life exactly what he promised in Matthew 4:19, but it required me to respond as Peter and James did in Matthew 4:20.

The things from Luke 14 became a reality in my life, but not in the way you might think. I didn't become a homeless bum who abandoned my family. What I did was to follow Jesus wherever He led me, regardless of how it looked for my family's financial stability or future. Many people, including Christians, accused me of neglecting my responsibility to provide for my family. To others, it looked like I hated my wife and kids.

Calling Jesus Lord means one thing: surrender to Him. It is an act of faith, but not a singular one. Like the electricity coming into your house, faith just keeps showing up. When a lamp is turned on, the electricity doesn't get to decide what to do, it simply responds to the switch flipping by lighting up the bulb. Faith means that I am as surrendered to God as the electricity is to the light switch.

Just as electricity continually flows into a home by a single power line that then delivers and disperses the electricity throughout the house, we enter into a life of faith with one act of surrender that continually allows God to call the shots in our lives.

Hearing God

In order for us to follow Jesus, we have to know where He is leading us. In John 10, Jesus tells us several things. He says that His sheep will hear His voice, they will know Him, and they follow Him. God wants us to hear Him and have us _know_ that He is speaking to us, so that we are able to follow Him. The pertinent question is how does God speak to us, and how do we know it's Him?

I think that a no so uncommon problem is that we are often unaware that we aren't listening to God. We don't even realize that we don't know how to listen to Him; we try to pray but end up monologuing to ourselves. We must learn how to listen to God. Instead of approaching Him with our plan, we must allow God to exchange our plan into His.

An essential part of hearing God is being willing to listen to and accept whatever He has to say. James 4:2-3 (WEB) says: "...*You don't have, because you don't ask. You ask, and don't receive, because you ask with wrong motives, so that you may spend it on your pleasures.*"

How often do our prayers involve us either trying to get God to do what we want or looking for the answers we want to hear? Is the goal of our prayers to find resolutions to our problems and answers to our questions that will make us comfortable and happy? I believe that one of the reasons we have a hard time hearing from God is that we often treat Him like a genie-in-a-bottle. We only listen for the answers we want to hear and consequently when He does speak, we aren't paying attention and we end up dismissing or ignoring what He says.

Over the next few chapters, we will look at how to hear God and how to prepare our hearts to listen to Him so that we can know how to follow Jesus on our faith journey.

Prayer

Prayer is where God prepares us to be able to listen to Him. Prayer causes us to get our heart in line with God's will so that we are better able to hear Him. In Matthew 6:6 (NKJV), Jesus said, *"But you, when you pray, go into your room, and when you have shut your door, pray to your Father who is in the secret place; and your Father who sees in secret will reward you openly."* Through prayer, God produces an inner change in our very nature that results in us naturally having different actions and behaviors.

Jesus went on in verses 9-13 (NKJV) and said:
"In this manner, therefore, pray:
  Our Father in heaven,
    Hallowed be Your name.
Your kingdom come,
  Your will be done,
    On earth as it is in heaven.
Give us this day our daily bread.

125

And forgive us our debts,
    As we forgive our debtors.
And do not lead us into temptation,
    But deliver us from the evil one.
For Yours is the kingdom
    And the power
        And the glory forever.
Amen."

Jesus was not telling us a specific prayer that God wants from us but was instead giving us an example of how to pray, with each individual section being the types of things we should pray through. How we do that, and what we pray changes over time as our relationship with God grows and changes. He was describing prayer as something that God uses to mold and shape us by conforming our attitude, thoughts, and desires to those of God so that we become a reflection of Him. Through prayer we surrender to God and to His will.

Our natural desire is to be self-reliant adults who can figure out everything on our own based on what makes sense to us, but Jesus called us to be like little children (Matthew 19:14). In prayer, we are taking a journey into our Father's presence. We come to Him like a child speaking to a parent Who loves us and knows what is best for us. We seek His wisdom and guidance in every facet of our lives, accepting that He knows what is best and that our decisions apart from Him tend to lead us astray.

One of the places that we tend to go astray, is when we rely on our own decision-making process, which is sin. Recently an older Christian lady asked me what the Bible has to say about her romantic relationship with a non-Christian. 2 Corinthians 6:14-18 teaches us that this type of relationship will constantly be trying to pull us away from God and will lead us down a road full of brokenness and sorrow. The lady I spoke with believed that she had to stay in the relationship because she thinks she can't control who she loves.

God placed a very clear warning in the Bible, yet the lady I spoke with based her decision on her emotions and wisdom rather than on what God has to say. Jeremiah 17:9 teaches us that our emotions are incredibly deceptive. The enemy used this lady's emotions as a weapon against her in order to deceive her, exactly as he did with Eve in the Garden of Eden.

Satan tries to convince us that our emotions define what is real. The lady I spoke with decided that her feelings for her boyfriend were truer than what God says. The sad reality is that she chose to do something that will make her feel good for a period of time but will eventually lead to substantial pain and heartache.

Proverbs 14:12 (WEB) *"There is a way which seems right to a man, but in the end, it leads to death."*

People are selfish and self-centered. We want what we want when we want it; giving little regard to the outcome. We tend to put our needs and desires before those of others. We want to be liked and popular. We aren't typically content with having our basic needs met but instead we usually want bigger, better things. Our natural disposition is so completely focused on self, that without some sort of intervention, we can't follow Jesus or live by faith.

Jesus said in Luke 9:23 (NKJV), *"If anyone desires to come after Me, let him deny himself, and take up his cross daily, and follow Me."* Prayer is where self-denial begins; it's where our heavenly Father changes our hearts, and gives us both the desire and ability to do to die to ourselves (Philippians 2:12-13).

Jesus said that God *openly* rewards prayer. In prayer, as we offer God control of our lives; our emotions, desires, pursuits, decision making, and everything else, the result is that God changes our very nature so that the way that we think and act line up with His will (Romans 12:2). Consequently, we increasingly become more like Jesus, and less like our old sinful selves.

Prayer is so important to faith because we naturally live for ourselves, and faith requires that we die to ourselves and live for God. God doesn't call us to live by faith, then leave us to do it by our own devices. He uses prayer to continually bring our heart and will into alignment with His so that obedience becomes our default.

The Bible

Psalm 119:105 says that God's Word is a lamp for our feet, and a light for our path. God speaks to us through the Bible. Hebrews 4:12 (NKJV) says: *"For the word of God is living and powerful, and sharper than any two-edged sword, piercing even to the division of soul and spirit, and of joints and marrow, and is a discerner of the thoughts and intents of the heart."* As you read the Bible, God will speak to you directly about your life and the things going on in it, prompting you to recognize and to deal with the deepest issues in your life, as well as providing direction on things you should do and how you should live.

The Holy Spirit Who lives inside of us gives us the desire and ability to respond in obedience to what He says to us through the Bible (Philippians 2:13) and transforms our character as we do (Romans 12:2).

Sometimes you will read something that gives you direction for your life, like when I read Ephesians 4:28 (March 2009). Sometimes when you read, God will use it to show you an area of sin in your life that you were unaware of. Sometimes when life doesn't make sense, you'll read a story of something God did in someone's life, and you'll realize that God is doing something similar in your life. When you are hurting or broken or need direction or answers, and we seek God through the Bible, He has an amazing way of telling us what we need, and it is often different than what we want.

When God tells us what we need through the Bible, it's not as simple as acquiring information. You find that when God speaks directly to you through the Bible, He makes the words come alive, and somehow you just understand the meaning of what you are reading in a way that is intimate to you. It's almost as if someone is giving you a detailed explanation of how the text applies to you and what you are to do with it. This is the Holy Spirit speaking clearly to you, giving you direction, wisdom, and help.

2 Timothy 3:16-17 (WEB) says: *"Every Scripture is God-breathed and profitable for teaching, for reproof, for correction, and for instruction in righteousness, that each person who belongs to God may be complete, thoroughly equipped for every good work"* The Bible was breathed out by God through human authors in a way similar to how God breathed the breath of life into Adam, which made Adam become a living being (Genesis 2:7).

While the Bible doesn't have a mind of its own as people do, it is a supernatural book that is living and active (Hebrews 4:12). The Holy Spirit works in our lives individually through the Bible. He tailors what we find in the Bible based on what He wants to say to us each individually. This does not imply that the meaning of the Bible is in flux or that people will hear things from God that contradict what He says to someone else. God can, however, say different things to different people through the same verses without ever being contradictory.

During creation, God said "let there be" multiple times and BOOM! Things instantly came into existence. The sun, moon, earth, plants, animals, water, stars, humans, and much, much more came into existence simply because God told it to. There is power in what God says that we can't even begin to understand. God breathed out the Bible through human authors, investing the same power into the Bible that He used to create everything. He uses that power to speak to us powerfully through the Bible.

If reading the Bible hasn't been a regular part of your life here are some tips to help you get started without feeling overwhelmed or lost.

Basic Bible Reading Tips
1. Read the Bible every day. If you miss a day, it's OK. Don't beat yourself up. God isn't upset with you at all.
   a. Setting a regular time for it every day is one of the most critical keys to consistency.
   b. Don't schedule days off

2. Start with one of the gospels (Matthew, Mark, Luke, John) and read all the way through. I recommend John
   a. The Gospels are all different accounts of the life of Jesus, and you want to get to know Him.

    b. Start at verse 1 chapter 1 and read each day until you feel like you've reached a stopping point.

    c. The next day pick up where you left off the previous day.

3. Pray before you read and ask God to speak to you and to give you understanding.

4. Read with the intent of listening to God and getting to know Him.

5. If it doesn't seem like you understand what you're reading or you aren't hearing from God, just keep going, it'll come to you.

    a. Psalm 119:130 (NKJV) says, "The entrance of Your Word gives light; it gives understanding to the simple."

    b. That means the more you read the Bible, the more you will understand it.

6. Get a journal of some type. Write down anything that grabs your attention or anything you have questions about.

    a. I use composition notebooks that cost about $1

7. Talk to people about what you're reading and what God is saying to you.

8. If you have a reading disability, try using an audio Bible.
   a. This doesn't apply if you simply don't like to read.

9. If reading is no trouble for you then use a physical Bible, or a Bible app.

10. There are three main types of Bible translations. They are literal, paraphrase, thought for thought.
    a. Literal (also known as word for word) is the most accurate type of translation. The goal of this type of translation is to stay as close as possible to the words and phrases used in the original language
       i. Literal translations best convey what the Bible says in its original languages.
       ii. Examples are NKJV, ESV, NASB.

       iii. NKJV is my personal favorite.

b. Thought for thought translations sacrifice some accuracy for the sake of readability.
       i. They tend to have a much higher word count than other translations.
       ii. Examples include NIV, NRSB

c. The main goal of paraphrase translations is readability. They attempt to capture the idea of what was written in the original languages at the cost of accuracy, meaning and context.
       i. While very easy to read, these translations greatly sacrifice what the Biblical authors were trying to say.
       ii. Examples include the NLT, TNIV

d. While some translations are more accurate than others, The Holy Spirit can speak to anyone through any translation of Bible.
       i. It is not possible to perfectly translate

from Hebrew and Greek into any other language.
ii. God's ability to communicate with us is not limited to our inability to perfectly translate.
iii. Find a translation that works for you and use it.
e. The Message is not a Bible translation. It is the author's personal interpretation of the Bible.
f. The Passion Translation is a bad mistranslation that adds things to the Bible that aren't in the original languages.

11. Study Bibles and Commentaries are OK, but you should try to read the Bible without them. Commentaries or study Bibles give you a person's opinion of what the Bible says. They may be correct, but it can keep you from hearing what God is trying to say to you.

God Also Speaks Through...

There are other ways that God speaks to us. Before we get into any of those, you must never forget that if you ever think you are hearing from God, and it contradicts *anything* the Bible says, then there is a 100% chance you aren't hearing God because everything in the Bible was said by God, and God never contradicts Himself.

It is also incredibly important to understand that the Bible is God's primary way of communicating with us. If you aren't primarily seeking Him in the Word, you won't know Him or know how to hear Him and will almost certainly misinterpret anything else He says to you, if you even hear Him at all. Not only that but you will likely think you hear Him when in fact you don't and will almost certainly be deceived into going astray down a path where

God was never leading you while believing that He was.

The Church
God will often speak to us through other believers in a variety of ways.

- When God called me to start a non-profit mechanic company, He spoke to me directly through a sermon.

- God will confirm things He tells us through other believers. Once God gave me a burden to plan and lead VBS for a church. Within two minutes, my middle daughter, unprompted, out of the blue, told me we needed to do VBS. The moment she stopped talking, my phone rang, and another leader at our church told me we should do VBS. We did VBS that year, and it was crazy amazing.

- God uses other believers to correct and encourage each other and to give counsel.

- God will give believers specific messages for other believers.

These are just some of the ways that God speaks to believers through other believers. There is no exhaustive list.

Directly through the Holy Spirit.

God will speak to us directly at times through the Holy Spirit. Acts 13 is a great Biblical example. At the church in Antioch, they were fasting and ministering to the Lord, and the Holy Spirit told the group that He was calling Saul and Barnabas to be missionary church planters. How exactly did The Holy Spirit speak? We don't know, but the passage plainly tells us that He spoke directly to them and that they absolutely knew it was the Holy Spirit speaking as well as what He was telling them. The Bible has multiple examples of times when God spoke directly to people, but I must point out that it's not the most common form of communication that we see God using.

There are multiple examples in the Bible of God speaking to people audibly. Just a few examples can be found in Exodus 3:14; Joshua 1:1; Judges 6:18; 1 Samuel 3:11; 2 Samuel

2:1; Job 40:1; Isaiah 7:3; Jeremiah 1:7; Acts 13.

This is something I've experienced a few times. The Guitar (April 11) is one of my favorites. The few times that God has spoken directly to me it's been an audible voice that I heard and immediately knew was God in the same way that I know when my wife of 24 years is speaking to me. When my wife says something to me, I don't have to stop and question whether or not it's her, I just know it is because I know her. Instead of trying to figure out if it's my wife, I just start engaging with her in the conversation. That's been my experience when God has spoken directly to me.

Every time I've heard God speak directly to me, it's always been in line with His character and never contradicted the Bible in any way. I've been asked how I knew for sure it was God speaking. In Luke 7:35 (KJV), Jesus said, *"But wisdom is justified of all her children."* In the last 12 years, I've heard God speak directly to me maybe five or six times, and I always responded in the same manner. When I look at the results, there always something that happened that would have been impossible apart from God.

Other Ways

God also speaks to believers at times through circumstances, coincidences, music, and our conscience. While God speaks through these means (and others) they can be subjective to interpretation based on how we feel. We must always remember that our emotions are very deceptive (Jeremiah 17:9), so if you think God is speaking to you in any of these ways, it needs to be verifiable through scripture in order to be valid.

Because God is God, He is all powerful and can speak to us through whatever way He sees fit. He could speak to someone through a talking donkey, a booming voice from heaven, or an odd-looking homeless guy on a street corner if He so chooses. The main point is that our hearts must get in line with God's if we are going to hear Him. We must be surrendered to God and listen to what He has to say if we are to be able to follow Jesus. If we follow Jesus, God will do amazing things in and through our lives and will lead people to Himself through us.

Conclusion

I spent the first 30 years of my life trying to do Christianity but ended up failing miserably. Once I surrendered to God, He began leading me on an amazing faith journey that has had an impact on where people will spend eternity. God has used my faith to change people's eternal destiny from hell to heaven.

Your Life can be a Crazy God Story...
Surrender to God... Listen to Him... Follow Jesus... Grow in Faith...

Blaze the Trail of Your Own Faith Journey with God...

Romans 12:2 (NKJV)
And do not be conformed to this
world, but be transformed by the
renewing of your mind, that you
may prove what is that good
and acceptable and perfect
will of God.

How can you allow God to transform
your mind?
The result of doing so is that you will
find yourself in the middle of God's
will...

Ephesians 2:10 (WEB)
For we are his workmanship, created
in Christ Jesus for good works,
which God prepared before
that we would walk
in them.

God has a plan for your life…

Philippians 2:13 (NKJV)
...for it is God who works in you both to will and to do for His good pleasure.

God who lives in us gives us both the desire and the ability to do the things that please Him.

Hebrews 12:1-2 (NKJV)

Therefore we also, since we are surrounded by so great a cloud of witnesses, let us lay aside every weight, and the sin which so easily ensnares us, and let us run with endurance the race that is set before us, looking unto Jesus, the author and finisher of our faith, who for the joy that was set before Him endured the cross, despising the shame, and has sat down at the right hand of the throne of God.

Philippians 2:12-13 (NKJV)

Be anxious for nothing, but in everything by prayer and supplication, with thanksgiving, let your requests be made known to God; and the peace of God, which surpasses all understanding, will guard your hearts and minds through Christ Jesus.

Thankfulness in prayer is one of the most effective weapons against anxiety.

Philippians 1:6 (MEV)

I am confident of this very thing, that He who began a good work in you will perfect it until the day of Jesus Christ.

God is never done with you.

Hebrews 4:16 (NKJV)
Let us therefore come boldly to the
throne of grace, that we may
obtain mercy and find
grace to help in
time of need.

Psalm 1:1-3 (NKJV)

1. Blessed is the man
Who walks not in the counsel
of the ungodly,
Nor stands in the path of
sinners,
Nor sits in the seat of the
scornful;
2. But his delight is in the law
of the Lord,
And in His law he meditates
day and night.
3. He shall be like a tree
Planted by the rivers of water,
That brings forth its fruit in its
season,
Whose leaf also shall not
wither;
And whatever he does
shall prosper.

The river is a symbol of
The Holy Spirit.
The person who love's
God's Word will be fed
by The Holy Spirit

Printed in Great Britain
by Amazon

18811561R00088